City Lights at Night

by Beth Fintan
illustrated by Meryl Henderson

Practice Decodable 63

Mc Graw Hill Education

Bothell, WA • Chicago, IL • Columbus, OH • New York, NY

MHEonline.com

Send all inquiries to:
McGraw-Hill Education
8787 Orion Place
Columbus, OH 43240

ISBN: 978-0-02-130358-8
MHID: 0-02-130358-4

Printed in China.

8 9 10 11 12 DSS 27 26 25 24 23

On nice nights, we do not sleep.
Dad, Mom, and I sail on the lake.

The night lights are bright.
A slight wind takes us out.

We sigh when we see the city.
The lights sparkle at night.

High up we see a plane in flight.
Its red lights blink.

The bright city lights glitter on a clear night.
They make a nice sight.

We like to sail at night.
We might sail next Friday night.